pizza

face

tablecloth

hat

1

Name _____

Consonants: **Pp, Ss**
Color, cut, and paste
in the correct column.

2

FS-32042 Reading

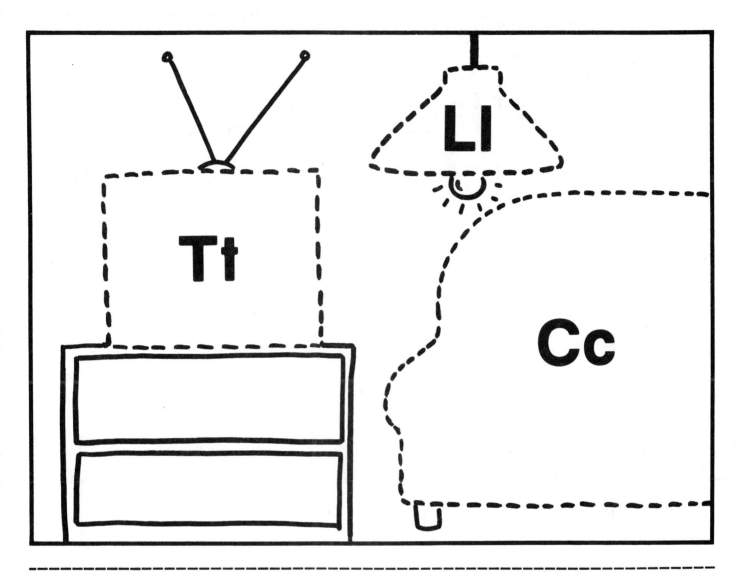

light

television

couch

Name _____

Consonants: **Ff, Tt**
Color, cut, and paste
in the correct column.

4

FS-32042 Reading

Name _____

Consonants: **Dd, Rr**
Color, cut, and paste
in the correct column.

Rr

Dd

© Frank Schaffer Publications, Inc.

FS-32042 Reading

Name _____

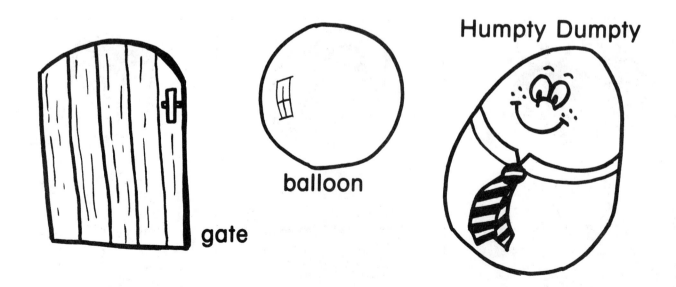

gate

balloon

Humpty Dumpty

6

Name _____

Consonants: **Bb, Ll**
Color, cut, and paste
in the correct column.

Bb

Ll

FS-32042 Reading

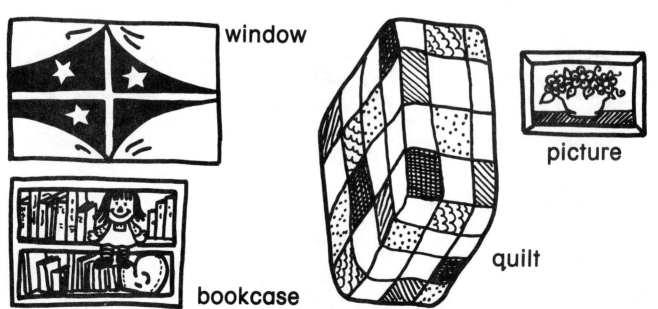

window

picture

quilt

bookcase

FS-32042 Reading

Name _____

Consonants: **Gg, Mm**
Color, cut, and paste
in the correct column.

Gg

Mm

Name _____

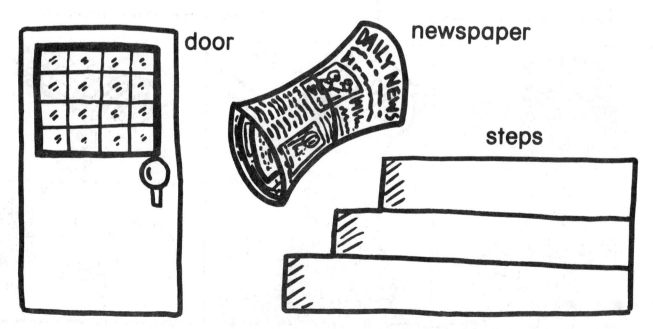

door

newspaper

steps

FS-32042 Reading

Name _____

Consonants: **Kk, Nn**
Color, cut, and paste
in the correct column.

FS-32042 Reading

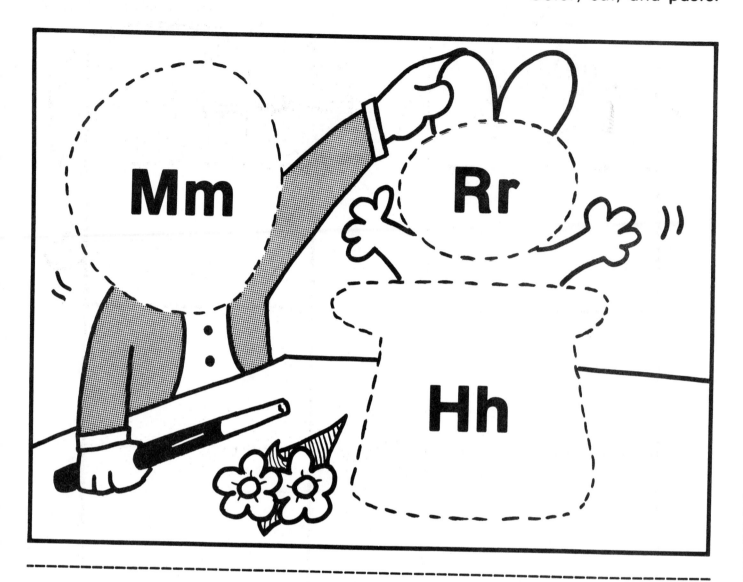

man

rabbit

hat

Name _____

Consonants: **Cc, Hh**
Color, cut, and paste
in the correct column.

FS-32042 Reading

Name _____

Consonants: **Vv, Ww**
Color, cut, and paste
in the correct column.

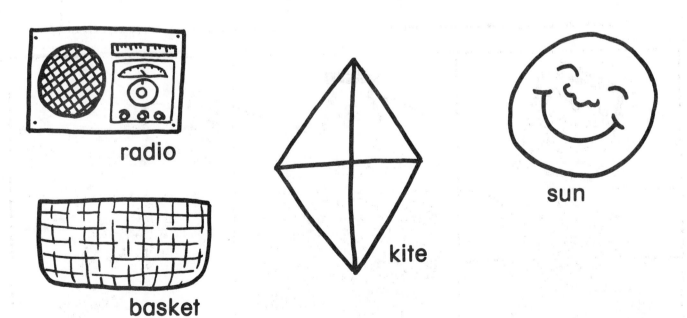

radio

basket

kite

sun

Name _____

diaper

mirror

playpen

wastebasket

Consonants: **Gg, Hh, Mm, Pp**
Color, cut, and paste.

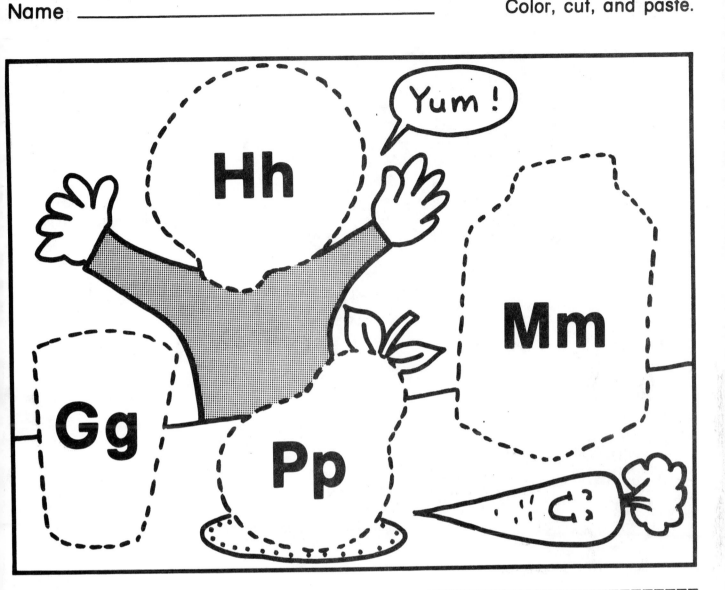

pear

milk

head

glass

FS-32042 Reading

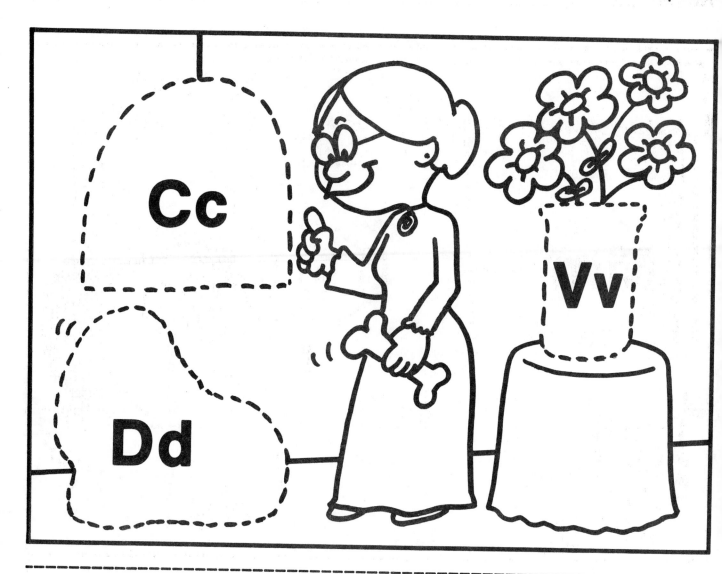

vase

dog

cage

FS-32042 Reading

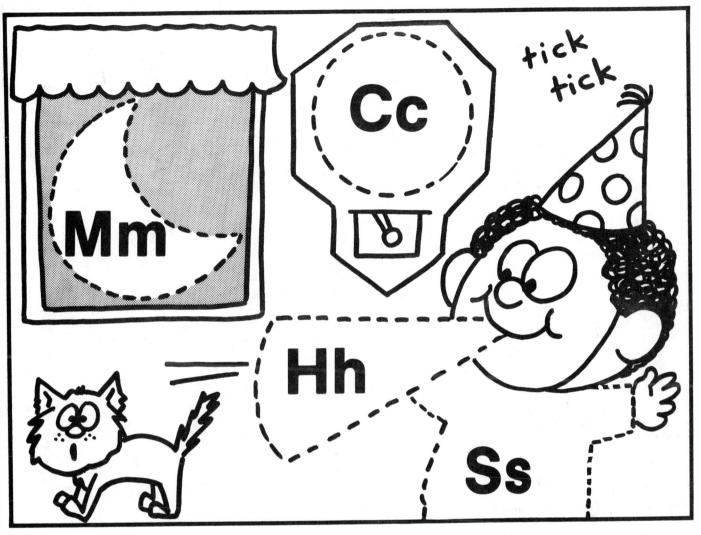

clock

moon

suit

horn

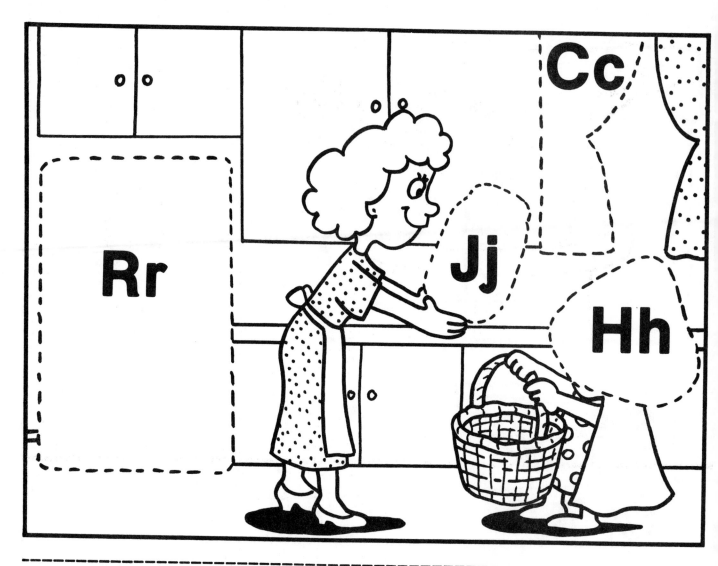

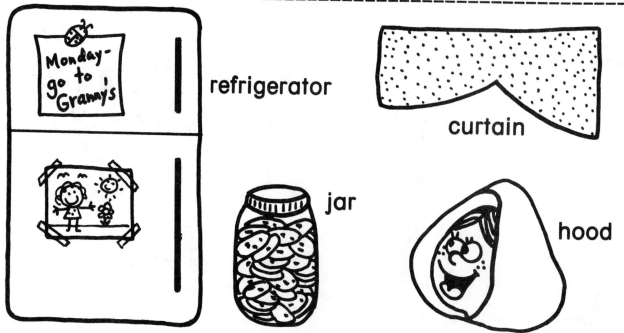

refrigerator

curtain

jar

hood

FS-32042 Reading

Name _____

in

out

 on

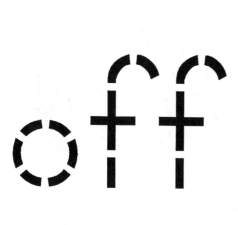

22

FS-32042 Reading

Skill: Discuss, trace and color.

cold

boy

girl

25

Name _____

up

down

FS-32042 Reading

Skill: Discuss, trace,
and color.

day

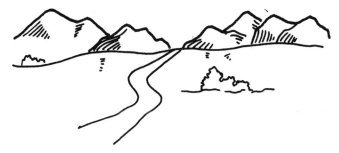

night

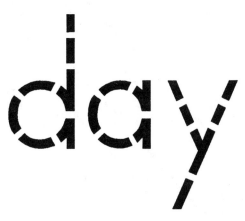

Name _____

sit

stand

28

push

pull

FS-32042 Reading

happy

sad

old

new

FS-32042 Reading

Skill: Discuss, trace
and colo

dry

wet

FS-32042 Reading

father

mother

Skill: Discuss, trace
and colo

cry

laugh

34

Skill: Discuss, trace, and color.

short

long

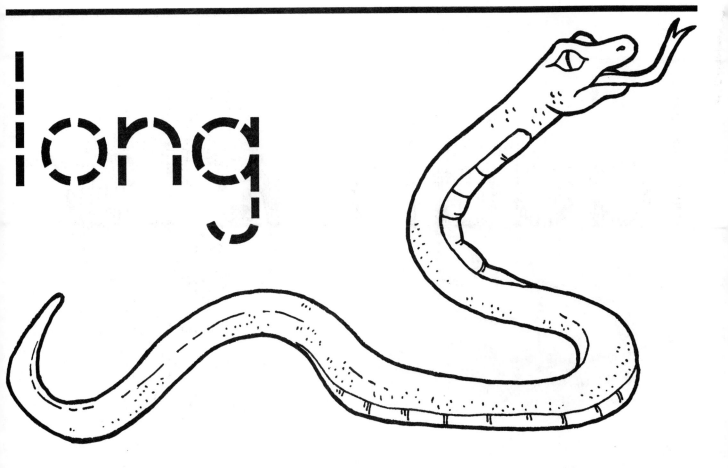

FS-32042 Reading

Skill: Discuss, trace, and color.

over

under

36

FS-32042 Reading

front

back

FS-32042 Reading

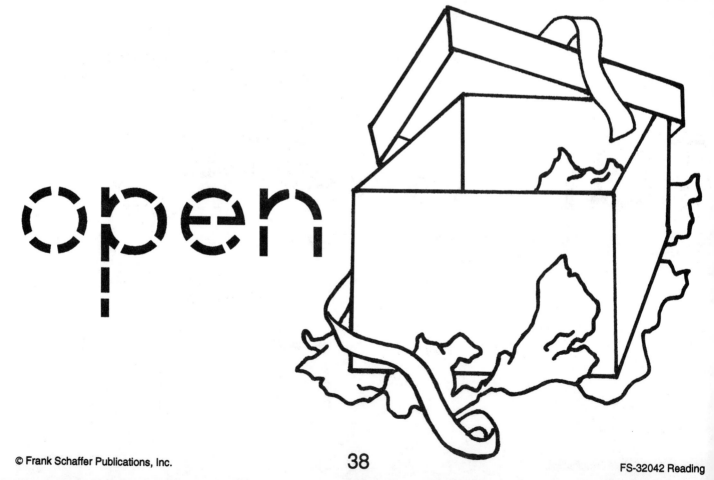

FS-32042 Reading

near

far

39

FS-32042 Reading

Skill: Discuss, trace
and color.

above

below

Name _____

What Comes Next?

Cut, match, and paste.

     FS-32042 Reading

Name _____

What Happened?

Cut, match, and paste.

Cause   Effect   Effect ✂

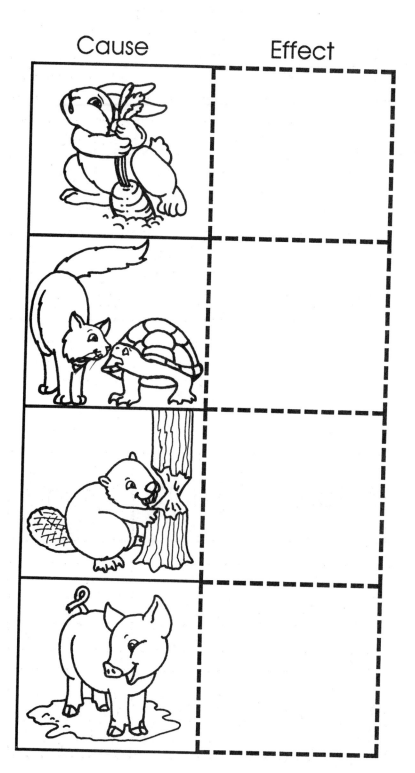

Name _____

Tricky Words

Color the pictures with words that are alike in each row.

43

Name _____

Animals

Cut, match, and paste.

Zoo

Pets

elephant   lion   dog   bear

cat   hamster   giraffe   parakeet

44

Name _____

Clothes

Cut, match, and paste.

Summer

Winter

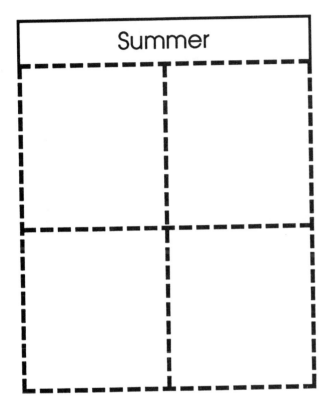
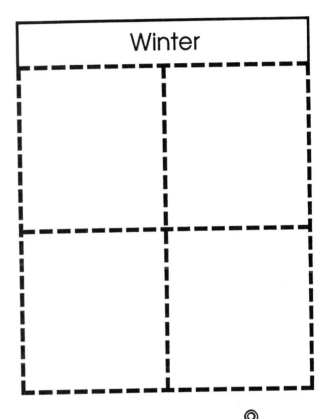

bathing suit	hat	sandals	scarf
mittens	sunglasses	boots	shorts

FS-32042 Reading

Name _____

Foods

Cut, match, and paste.

Fruits

Vegetables

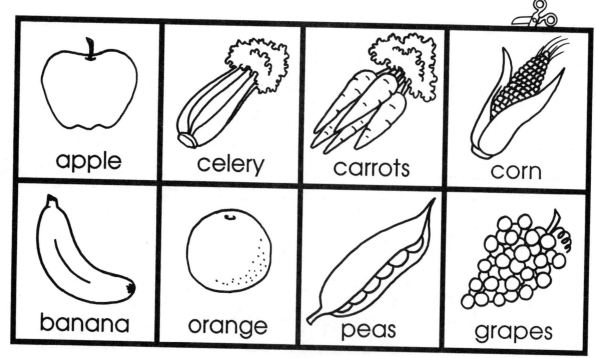

apple	celery	carrots	corn
banana	orange	peas	grapes

FS-32042 Reading

Name _____

Go-Togethers

Cut, match, and paste.

 is to  as  is to

 is to  as  is to

 is to 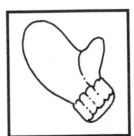 as 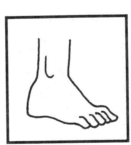 is to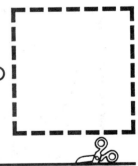

  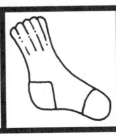

FS-32042 Reading

Name _____

What Goes Together?

Cut, match, and paste.

 is to 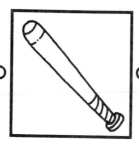 as [ ] is to

 is to  as [ ] is to

 is to  as  is to

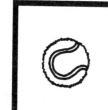  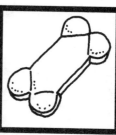

48

The Little People Study
Red

This book belongs to _____

FS-32042 Reading

Practice.

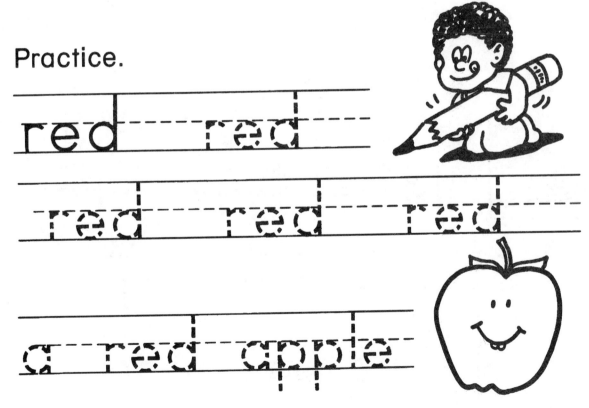

red   red

red   red   red

a red apple

1

FS-32042 Reading

See the red wagon.

2

FS-32042 Reading

See the red flowers.

3

FS-32042 Reading

Color all the spaces marked **red** with a red 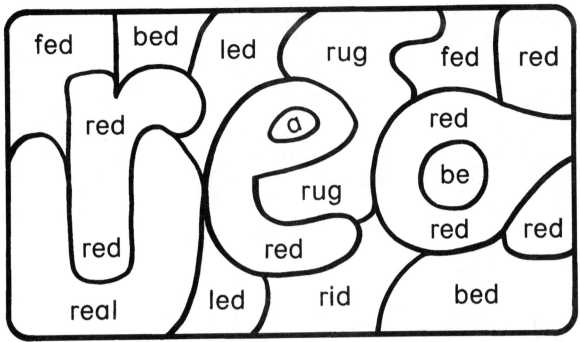. Color other spaces green.

fed bed led rug fed red
red a red
rug be
red red red
red
real led rid bed

Fill-in.

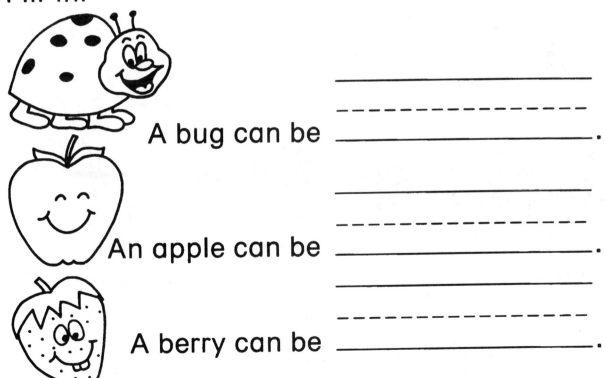

A bug can be _____ .

An apple can be _____ .

A berry can be _____ .

Green

This book belongs to _____

FS-32042 Reading

Practice.

green green

green green

a green frog

1

FS-32042 Reading

Grass can be green.

2

See the green frogs!

3

We are green.

Fill in.

A leaf can be _____
_____.

A worm can be _____
_____.

Are you green? _____
_____

The Little People Study
Yellow

This book belongs to _____

FS-32042 Reading

See the yellow chicks.

1

FS-32042 Reading

Practice.

yellow yellow

yellow yellow

yellow paint

See the yellow flowers.

Find the word **yellow**. Color it yellow!

Fill in.

The sun can be _____.

A chick can be _____.

A lemon can be _____.

The Little People Study
Blue

This book belongs to _____

FS-32042 Reading

The sky is blue.

1

FS-32042 Reading

See the blue water.

Fill in.

_____

Water can be _____ .

A bird can be _____ .

Are you blue? _____

The Little People Study
Brown

This book belongs to _____

FS-32042 Reading

See the brown dog.

1

FS-32042 Reading

Practice.

brown   brown

brown   brown

a   brown   bunny

    2   FS-32042 Reading

See the brown worms.

    3   FS-32042 Reading

Color the things that are often brown.

Fill in.

A bear can be _____.

Ice cream can be _____.

Worms can be _____.

The Little People Study
Purple

This book belongs to _____

  FS-32042 Reading

Practice.

purple   purple

purple   purple

a purple plum

1 FS-32042 Reading

We are purple.

Fill-in.

Grapes can be _____.

Jam can be _____.

Are you purple? _____

The Little People Study
Black

This book belongs to _____

   FS-32042 Reading

It is night!

The night sky is black.

1   FS-32042 Reading

My bear is black.

Practice.

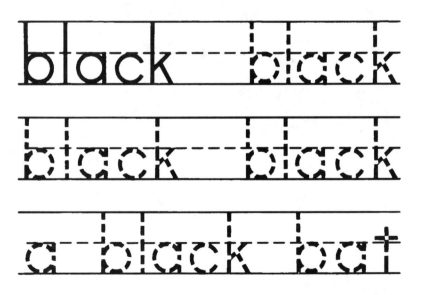

The Little People Study
Orange

This book belongs to _____

FS-32042 Reading

Hi, Fred.

My fish is orange.

1

FS-32042 Reading

I see an orange.

FS-32042 Readi

Practice.

orange   orange

orange   orange

an orange carrot

FS-32042 Readi

Ben Can See!

This book belongs to _____

  FS-32042 Reading

I see a cat.

1 FS-32042 Reading

I see a bat.

     2   FS-32042 Readin

I see a bug.

     3   FS-32042 Reading

I see a rat.

4

FS-32042 Reading

I see a bee.

5

FS-32042 Reading

Practice:

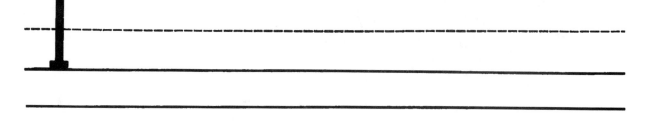

I

a

see

Match:

1. I see a **bug**.

2. I see a **cat**.

3. I see a **bee**.

4. I see a **rat**.

5. I see a **bat**.

Peg Can See!

This book belongs to _____

     FS-32042 Reading

See the hole.

1   FS-32042 Reading

See the snake.

2

FS-32042 Reading

See the egg.

3

FS-32042 Reading

See the bird.

4

FS-32042 Reading

I see a girl.

See the bug.

5

FS-32042 Reading

Trace:

see see see see

the the the the

can can can can

6 FS-32042 Reading

Circle the matching words in each row:

see	bee see saw see see
the	the two the to the
can	can cap can ran can

7 FS-32042 Reading

We Can Swim!

This book belongs to _____

Frank Schaffer Publications, Inc.

Do you see the fish?

© Frank Schaffer Publications, Inc.

Yes, I see the fish!

Do you see the sea horse?

Yes, I see the sea horse.

Do you see the seal?

Practice:

do

you

yes

Write **yes** or **no.**

1. Do you see a ___?

2. Do you see a ___?

3. Do you see a ___?

4. Do you see a ___?

5. Do you see a ___?

I Can Do It!

This book belongs to _____

 FS-32042 Reading

Can you fly, Peg?

1 FS-32042 Reading

Yes, I can fly!

2

Can you jump, Ben?

3

Yes, I can jump.

I can.

I can.

Peg can dance. Can you?

Match:

yes   you

you   can

no   yes

can   no

Peg   Ben

Ben   Peg

    6   FS-32042 Reading

Write **yes** or **no**.

1. Can you fly?   _____

2. Can you swim?   _____

3. Can you run?   _____

4. Can you sleep?   _____

5. Can you dance?   _____

    7   FS-32042 Reading

Do You Like To Play?

This book belongs to _____

FS-32042 Reading

Do you like to jump?

1

FS-32042 Reading

Yes, I do like to jump.

Do you like to play ball?

No, I do not like to play ball.

4 FS-32042 Reading

Do you like to eat?

5 FS-32042 Reading

Match:

to ———————	do
no	— to
do	not
like	no
not	you
yes	like
you	yes

Write **yes** or **no**.

1. Do you like to eat?

2. Do you like to run?

3. Do you like to sleep?

4. Do you like to jump?

5. Do you like to eat bugs?

I Like To Eat.

This book belongs to _____

FS-32042 Reading

I am a rabbit.
I like to eat carrots.

1

FS-32042 Reading

I am a bug.
I like to eat leaves.

2 FS-32042 Reading

I am a bird.
I like to eat worms.

3 FS-32042 Reading

I am a rat.
I like to eat cheese.

I am a dog.
I like to eat meat.

Practice these words:

am   like   eat

Match:

I am a   I eat

I am a   I eat

I am a    I eat

I am a    I eat

I am a    I eat

I Like This!

This book belongs to_____

                    FS-32042 Reading

This is Peg.
I like Peg.

1   FS-32042 Reading

This is a snail.
I like this snail.

2

FS-32042 Reading

This is a spider.
Do you like this spider?

3

FS-32042 Reading

This is a turtle.
Do you like this turtle?

4 FS-32042 Reading

This is a snake.
I like this snake.

5 FS-32042 Reading

Write the right
word on the line.

cat dog bug rat

This is a _____.

This is a _____.

This is a _____.

This is a _____.

Draw a picture in
each box.

I like this.

I can do this.

I can eat this.

I do not like this.

I Love You!

This book belongs to _____

This is my mom.
My mom is big.

1

I love my mom.
My mom loves me.

This is my dad.
My dad is little.

I love my dad.
My dad loves me.

This is my dog.
I love my dog!

Draw:

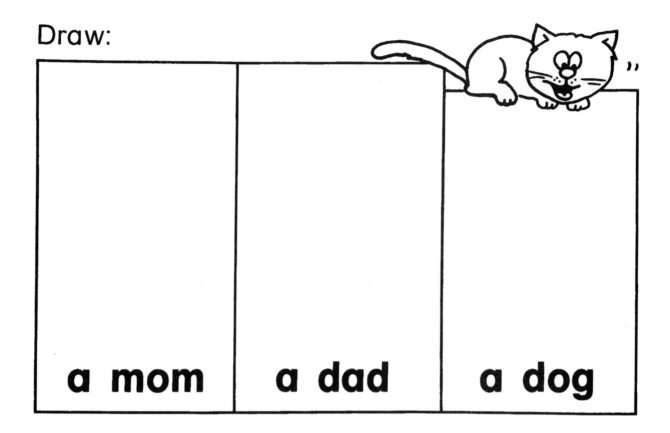

a mom	**a dad**	**a dog**

6 FS-32042 Reading

Practice:

big **little** **love**

7 FS-32042 Reading

Pets!

This book belongs to _____

FS-32042 Reading

Do you see my pet cat?
My cat is big!

1

FS-32042 Reading

This is my pet bug.
I love this little bug!

2 FS-32042 Reading

I do not see my pet bug!
Do you see my little bug?

3 FS-32042 Reading

This is not a pet!
This is a bee!

I love pets!
Do you like pets too?

Write **yes** or **no** on the line.

1. Is this a **cat?**  _____.

2. Is this a **rat?**  _____.

3. Is this a **bat?** _____.

4. Is this a **dog?**  _____.

5. Is this a **bug?** _____.

6 FS-32042 Reading

Write **big** or **little** on the line.

7 FS-32042 Reading

We Like To Dance!

This book belongs to _____

FS-32042 Reading

This is Peg.
We like to dance and dance!

1

FS-32042 Reading

This is my mom.
She likes to dance too!

2

FS-32042 Reading

This is my dad.
He likes to eat.

3

FS-32042 Reading

Do you see my pet bug?
She likes to dance too!

4 FS-32042 Reading

We do!

Me too!

We do!

I eat.

We like to dance.
Do you like to dance too?

5 FS-32042 Reading

Practice:

we   she   he

6

Match:

cat and dog

cat and rat

bat and rat

bug and dog

bug and cat

7

The Little People Study
Birds

This book belongs to _____

FS-32042 Reading

Birds have two legs.

1

FS-32042 Reading

Birds have beaks.

Look.

Birds have feathers.

Some birds can fly.

Color only the birds.

A duck is a bird.

Word Bank	fur	yes	fly
	feathers	no	two

Fill in.

1. Birds have _____.

2. Birds have _____ legs.

3. Some birds can _____.

4. Are you a bird? _____.

The Little People Study
Insects

This book belongs to _____

I am an insect.

Insects have six legs.

Some insects can fly.

Insects are all around.

Color only the insects.

4

FS-32042 Reading

Some insects are pests.

5

FS-32042 Reading

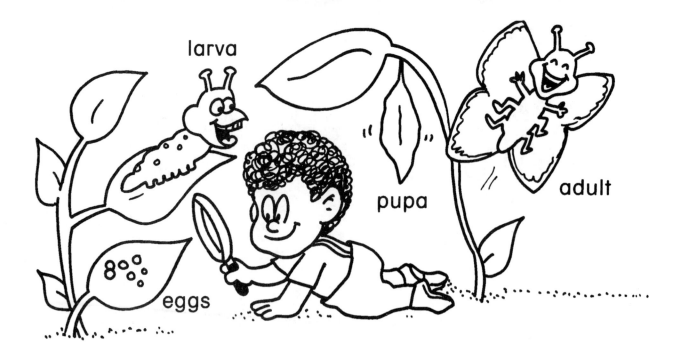

larva

pupa

adult

eggs

Some insects change.

6   FS-32042 Reading

Word Bank	yes	no	pests
	fly	six	two

Fill in.

1. Insects have _____ legs.

2. Some insects can _____.

3. Some insects are _____.

4. Are you an insect? _____.

7   FS-32042 Reading

The Little People Study
Reptiles and Fish

This book belongs to _____

FS-32042 Reading

No feathers!

Reptiles have scales.

1

FS-32042 Reading

Snakes and lizards are reptiles.

2

FS-32042 Reading

Dinosaurs were reptiles.

3

FS-32042 Reading

Fish live in water.

Fish breathe under water.

Fish have scales.

Word Bank	yes	no	reptile
	gills	water	fish

Fill in.

1. Fish breathe under _____.

2. Fish have _____.

3. Do reptiles have fur? _____.

4. A snake is a _____.

The Little People Study

Amphibians

toad

frog

This book belongs to _____

FS-32042 Reading

I have gills and breathe like a fish now!

A tadpole!

eggs

larva

Amphibians are born in water.

1

FS-32042 Reading

Amphibians grow legs.

Then amphibians breathe air.

We are amphibians, too.

Cut and paste in order on the next page. ✂

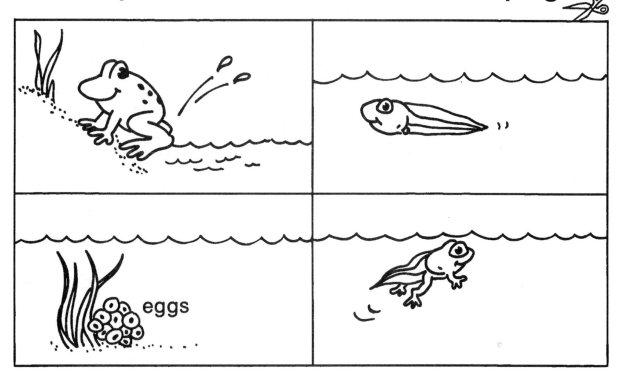

eggs

Paste pictures from the page before in order.

1	2
3	4

Metamorphosis

6 FS-32042 Reading

Word Bank	air	yes	hair
	water	no	legs

Fill in.

1. Amphibians are born in _____.

2. Amphibians grow _____.

3. Then amphibians breathe _____.

4. Are you an amphibian? _____

7 FS-32042 Reading

The Little People Study
Mammals

This book belongs to _____

FS-32042 Reading

Mammals have fur.

1

FS-32042 Reading

Mammals give milk.

2

FS-32042 Reading

A rabbit is a mammal.

3

FS-32042 Reading

An elephant is a mammal.

You are a mammal!

Draw a big mammal.

Color only the mammals.